# SHEEP THRILLS

## Life Lessons from Our Woolly Friends

Ewegenie R. Woolsey

PETER PAUPER PRESS, INC.
WHITE PLAINS, NEW YORK

To all of ewe who have
made this book possible

Designed by Taryn R. Sefecka

Photo credits appear on last page.

Visit us at www.peterpauper.com

# SHEEP THRILLS

## Life Lessons from Our Woolly Friends

# Introduction

Sheep are like ewe and me,
maybe just not as woolly-headed.

This tribute to our fluffy friends highlights their many ewe-nique traits. Sheeps' friendsheeps last a lifetime. They can tell a darn good yarn, stringing it out for hours. They are outstanding (and upstanding) in their fields. They can pull the wool over your eyes. They can ram their point home when it comes to debating the issues. Like you and me, they've probably got more than one black sheep in the family. And if you get them angry, they're sure to lamb-aste you.

Their credo:    Life's got plenty of mutton, and
                mutton's good enough for me.

As ruminating ruminants go, sheep can figure things out
pretty well; it just takes them more time than it would take
ewe. In any case, there are many lessons to be learned from
our woolly friends.

And for shear madness, nothing bleats a sheep!

The Editors

# I've only got eyes for ewe.

All the world loves a lover.

# Got cud?

Feast today. Fast tomorrow.

If you obey all the rules,
you miss all the fun.

KATHARINE HEPBURN

Ewe are totally ewe-nique.

# And the bleat goes on . . .

Once you make a decision, the universe conspires to make it happen.

RALPH WALDO EMERSON

Black sheep of

Remember, if people talk behind your back, it only means you are two steps ahead.

FANNIE FLAGG

the family

# Wait a minute while I consult the Ram-a-Sutra.

If you aren't going all the way, why go at all?

JOE NAMATH

# I've got ewe, babe.

Love is a verb.

EILEEN FLANAGAN

# Ewe've been fleeced!

Don't be frustrated by your inexperience—
all green things inevitably grow.

BETH MENDE CONNY

# Leadersheep at its best.

Leap, and the net will appear.

JULIA CAMERON

# What are ewe looking at?

Far too many people are looking for the right person,
instead of trying to be the right person.

GLORIA STEINEM

When the chips are
down, your family
is there to pick
up the pieces.

27

# Dalai Lamba says:

# "Find shear bliss. Become one with the herd."

Live in harmony with those around you.

# Smile for the camera—don't be sheepish!

I would rather sing one day
as a lion than 100 years as a sheep.

CECILIA BARTOLI

# Ewe rule!

Don't strive to be better than others; strive to be your best self.

BETH MENDE CONNY

Until you make peace with who you are,
you'll never be content with what you have.

DORIS MORTMAN

# Sheep in heavenly peace.

# Look at all the lonely sheeple.

It is in the company of a good friend that the heart finds a home.

BETH MENDE CONNY

# Ewe-l-tide greetings. Fleece Navidad.

I will honor Christmas in my heart, and try to keep it all the year.

CHARLES DICKENS

It's kind of fun to do the impossible.

WALT DISNEY

# Ever feel wild and woolly?

# Ewe are outstanding in your field.

They're cloning sheep. Great! Just what we need!
Sheep that look more alike than they already do!

DAVE BARRY

Let your dreams
be the springboard
for great actions.

LIESL VAZQUEZ

One day
my sheep will
come in.

One of my rules is:
Never try to do anything.
Just do it.

ANI DIFRANCO

No "ifs," "ands," or "butts" about it.

# Don't pull the wool over my eyes.

Fool me once, shame on you. Fool me twice, shame on me.

# Darn! I lost my spacesheep.

If you are lost, remember—you have merely
taken a detour on the way to your destination.

LYNNE AMES

Be comfortable with who you are.

# That's a sheep joke.

He who laughs, lasts.

Every ending is a new beginning.

# Photo Credits